YOUR COUNTRY IS GREAT
AFGHANISTAN–GUYANA

FUTUREPOEM BOOKS
NEW YORK CITY
2008

YOUR COUNTRY IS GREAT
AFGHANISTAN–GUYANA

ARA SHIRINYAN

FIRST EDITION | FIRST PRINTING

This edition first published in paperback by Futurepoem books
www.futurepoem.com
Series Editor: Dan Machlin
Guest Editors: Robert Fitterman, Tonya Foster, Laura Elrick

Design: Anthony Monahan (am@anthonymonahan.com)

Interior Cover Image scanned from historic map of unknown origin found by A. Shirinyan

Typesetting: Garrett Kalleberg

Cover set in Akzidenz-Grotesk and text set in Scala.
Printed in the United States of America on acid-free paper.
Signature Book Printing, www.sbpbooks.com

Futurepoem books is a New York City-based publishing collaborative dedicated to presenting innovative
works of contemporary poetry and prose by both emerging and important underrepresented writers.
Our rotating editorial panel shares the responsibility for selecting, designing and promoting the books we
produce. Futurepoem also occasionally invites writers or multi-genre artists to produce work for special
projects that is then documented in print or via other media.

This project is supported by an award from the New York State Council on the Arts, a State
Agency, the New York Community Trust, the Fund for Poetry, and Individual Donors.
Futurepoem receives nonprofit sponsorship for grants and donations through Fractured Atlas
Productions, Inc., a 501(c)3 tax exempt organization. Contributions are fully tax-deductible and
much needed!

NYSCA
New York State Council on the Arts

Distributed to the trade by Small Press Distribution, Berkeley, California
Toll-free number (U.S. only): 800.869.7553
Bay area/International: 510.524.1668
orders@spdbooks.org
www.spdbooks.org

I started making this book about three years ago, working on a few random countries: Mongolia, Kenya, Albania. Initially, I hadn't entertained the idea of making it exhaustive, going through the globe, etc. I was working on *Syria Is in the World* at the time and doing minor things on the side. I sent some of these poems to Stan Apps and he urged me to continue. He wrote a sort of review/essay on them for his blog. I gathered most of the material for what is now this book during one long weekend in September 2006. Editing it took many more months, but once I had the material for the book, I was happy.

For this project (this book being roughly the first third), I stuck to the list of countries and territories listed on the CIA's *The World Factbook* (2006 version). I would print out a page from the *Factbook*'s "Flags of the World" chapter and go to work. Using Google, I would type "[country] is great" and search. The quotes ensured that I would get any instance of those three words on the internet. If there are pages where nothing but the title exists, it's because nothing came up for those countries at the time I searched. That is, no one who could write in English and had access to the web thought to say anything great about those countries. Sometimes I would get very few results, at other times I would get dozens and dozens of pages. For those countries that brought up very few results I have done my best to make use of everything that came up. For those countries that gave hundreds of pages of results, there came a moment when I thought that I had enough to work with and stopped.

All the misspellings, irregular capitalization, and punctuation inconsistencies are as I found them. As I read through the rough collected material, I occasionally deleted results that did not fit whatever idea I had about the piece. The line breaks are mostly rhythmic and Rob Fitterman's suggestions toward this end were very helpful.

for Stan Apps,

friend and pusher

AFGHANISTAN IS GREAT

Afghanistan is great, but much smaller
than previously assumed.

the need for education
in Afghanistan is great
and must be met quickly,

need for food in Afghanistan is great,

well-acquainted
with unique problems
facing Afghanistan.

The need for tough, dependable,
locally repairable wheelchairs in
Afghanistan is great.

A mountain. An airplane. Aviation in
Afghanistan is great fun.

Pipeline via Afghanistan is great.

There is no question that Allah's
knowledge and love of Afghanistan
is great
even as he regrets
the limits of his understanding.

ALBANIA IS GREAT

Albania is great. I missed that place a lot.
I got offered cigarettes and alcohol by
like everyone I knew
and some people I didn't know.

Albania is great!
Not quite as third-world
as parts of Africa, but
not exactly Michigan either
if ykwim.

I liked everything about my stay
and i just wanted to let you know
that Albania is GREAT!!!

Albania is great as a communsist country
or democratic,
either way,
albania is just the best.

U aint from belgrade,
youd feel our pain and not
say how albania is great.
educate ur self:

Hiking, camping,
mountain-climbing,
hunting -- North
Albania is great
for all of this.

The Italian influence in Albania is great,
many speak Italian,
watch Italian TV.
The historical ties between Italy and Albania
are very strong.

I know you love your country but please
stop telling us that Albania is great. Like I said,
give us the worldly achievements of Albania.

Albania is great!!!!
We finished 5th place
because we were all injured.
And we lost against Georgia twice before
because we felt bad on those
two day's!

ALGERIA IS GREAT

hey how are you , algeria is great and sorry that
i cant talk to you . but my uncle has a cafe with
a bunch of computers . but i cant stay on to long

The basis of that construction primarily rests--better
said, they rested--on recovering Algeria is great natural
resources, These essentially were energy

Potentials for organic agriculture in Algeria is great.
Kabylia mountain region of about 100000 areas can
be converted to organic agriculture.

ANDORRA IS GREAT

One of Europe's smallest countries,
Andorra is great for skiing.
Montserrat Crazy mountain
with startling
naturally formed shapes
to give you the creeps.

The weather in Andorra is great
if you don't like it too cold

Andorra is great country to go shoping
since it is tax free you get lots of things
more cheaper than surraunding countries.
Alcohol, Parfumes,

Andorra is great place to do some winter sports,
they have lovely high mountains
you to ski or snowboard.
In the summer time you can go hiking

Andorra is great for cheap electrical goods
and there are perfume shops
everywhere you look.
Andorra is also great for its
spectacular views

I've been told the skiing in Andorra is great,
but I will write a 'winter' opinion on Andorra,
at a later date
ie when I've actually tried it out!

Andorra is great , snowboarding every day
(untill I broke my shoulder . . . duh !)
I wouldn ' t mind going back there .

ANGOLA IS GREAT

I hear western Angola is great this time of year.

The challenge faced by the media
and the institutions that have committed themselves
to supporting democracy in Angola
is great.

With all 12 nations enjoying free-market economies
and either full democracies or in the process of becoming
democratic, the potential for Angola is great.

sale of the 203-acre Oakhill Campground &
Retreat Center in Angola is great news for its
former owner, AG Financial of Springfield, Mo

i like your style...dig the tunes...Angola is great

ANGUILLA IS GREAT

anguilla is great for snorkeling
anguilla is a coral island in the
north eastern caribbean
anguilla is a british territory
in the caribbean

Anguilla is Great for Snorkeling
Anguilla is great for investment info
Carnival in Anguilla is Great.

All in all, Anguilla is great.
Great people,
great food,
great beaches.

ANTIGUA AND BARBUDA IS GREAT

ARGENTINA IS GREAT

Argentina is great. The food was truly one of the best finds.
The food is great - fresh and not spicy.
Not what most people from the US would expect.

I think Argentina is great for all kinds of stuff.
As it's such a big country, they have lots of thing
to do and see.
Argentina is great, and I want to make it grow,
grow and grow

Argentina is great - before I knew there was a shelter there,
I thought those ruins looked like the ultimate cat playground

Argentina is great because the population is 90-95% Meditteranean!
Few jews because the great Rightist pro-white military junta
got rid of 50k leftist jews
This is why I think the launching of legitimate services in Argentina
is great news."

Airbag, pop band, Argentina. "We are young and love music.
to have basically the biggest scores of the tournament
and to beat Argentina, is great,
such a relief to be in the quarter-finals.

Argentina is great and might have had an edge,
but they still lost, Which is what counts.
To call them talentless is insane
and disrespectful

Following the devaluation of the peso,
shopping in Argentina is great for tourists
who can get a lot for the money.

Argentina is great
but the way they do business here
is criminal. There is a reason

they are ranked as one of the most corrupt countries in the world.
Birdwatching in Argentina is great
Argentina is great for that
and cheap at it

I like meat, so Argentina is GREAT.
Lots of BEEF.

This garlicky sauce from Argentina is great
spooned over beef or chicken.

what an original argument:
argentina is shit.
argentina is great.
get over yourselves and accept the truth;
argentina is both of those things,

ARMENIA IS GREAT

armenia is great country
famous for its christianity!

Armenia is great, and Yerevan is a city
where people live their lifes to the maximum
I love you Yerevan,
I love your streets,
your sidewalks,

Armenia is great
everyone should go back
at least once

the new information on Armenia is great –
lots of good information –
I'll have to remember not to give
anyone 2 flowers!

I also do not speak our language
Armenia is great though.
I have been there
and made good friends,
even though I could not
speak a word to them.

Tour to Armenia is a great success!
To Understand Our
Past,
Is To Understand
Ourselves.

renovated sidewalks, roads, and
unprecedented High Rise buildings
going up
the future of Armenia is great.

With such warm summers
and very cold winters
you will learn a great deal
about the history of Yerevan

Armenia is great
I love it, but I dont think
it is for me.

ARUBA IS GREAT

aruba is great
its beaches are beautiful
and the people are great

Aruba is great for diving
and seeing marine life
with visibility up to 90 ft.
You will see sponge tubes,
gliding manta rays, sea turtles, lobsters,

The taxi service on Aruba is great,
but we like to pick up and go wherever
and whenever we want,
so the rental is great for us.

Aruba is great for sightseeing, shopping,
and a variety of water sports.
You should plan on renting a car
to explore the island.

Aruba is great,
not a drop of rain,
barely a cloud
and yet
never felt too hot

Aruba is great,
that is where i went
on my honeymoon last year.
I love it!
There are many places to stay.
The Marriott is nice,
the Wyndham is nice.

Aruba is great for singles,
couples and families.

Probably the best miniature golf courses
in the world
are in Aruba

Aruba is great for a honeymoon
for the following reasons:
1. No hurricanes
2. Predictable weather
3. Tons to do

Aruba is great.
If you bust out early,
be sure to go snorkelling.
They have a party bus
for bar hopping

AUSTRALIA IS GREAT

Australia is great
Not many
people,
beautiful landscape.

I think Australia is great because we
have no wars and no fighting. Our
peaceful life in Australia is great.
We are not stressed or worried

Australia is great because
we accept each other
without rhyme or reason.
It doesn't matter

Extra note:
Shopping in Australia is great,
since the exchange rate
is very favorable to
the American dollar

The long-term future of Australia
is great,
especially if India and China progress.
If the average consumer in Asia
is allowed
to buy a car
and a house

Australia is great at producing knowledge-based companies
with innovative ideas
and strong export potential

Fruit picking in Australia is great exercise
and can be physically demanding.

Fruit picking in Australia can also often involve
spending a lot of time up a ladder

Australia is great,
but nothing I did when working
was valued.

Australia is great for solo travelers
Australia, is great for fishing
Australia is great if you have that City class dog
Australia is great for ripping up the dirt on a set of wheels

Yes Australia is great - I love living here.
I'm sure its a little different to Oklahoma,
although probably more similar than you might think.

AUSTRIA IS GREAT

The real winner in Austria is great skiing
and everything else, the huts on the mountains,
the ski bars,
restaurants,
clubs,
the atmosphere

Austria is great. The Alps are really amazing.
Snowboarding in Insbruck is the best,
Vienna is quite a lovely city.
Austria is Austria

Austria is great for families...
so I took mine!
This year our family decided to combine my work
with vacation,
so we all went to Austria.

Anyway, Austria is great
except no one likes someone
who can only speak American English,
I don't like being in a place where I
have to have a translater

Austria is great for Christmas.
Apart from the skiing
the whole atmosphere
is just so
atmospheric

If you have the legs for the hills
and the stomach for the schnitzel,
Austria is great bicycling country.

AZERBAIJAN IS GREAT

Azerbaijan is great these days
Azerbaijan is great ty for asking
Azerbaijan is great! I like it!
thanks for sharing :smile:

The importance of Midia ,
its cultural heritage
in the history ,
especially in the history
of Azerbaijan is great .
More than a two - century existence

Armed Forces of Pakistan to Azerbaijan
is great honor for them
Azerbaijan has great cooperation
potential with China

Potential for the development of tourism
in Azerbaijan is great:
favorable natural-climatic conditions,
resort area on the coast of the Caspian sea

The Naxcivan Autonomous
Republic is a great vacation
spot if you don't mind the
constant menace of Armenia

the potential for elimination
of water deficiency
in Azerbaijan is great and expected
amounts of water deficiency with
climate change can be reduced

Nation of Azerbaijan is great.
We are 50 millions. This is big
nation in the world scale.

All we have one Homeland –
Azerbaijan. We must try to strengthen

Azerbaijan is great these days
Azerbaijan is great ty for asking
Azerbaijan is great! I like it!
thanks for sharing :smile:

THE BAHAMAS IS GREAT

Shark diving in the Bahamas
is great for all levels of divers.

The diving in the Bahamas is great!
The water is warm and clear

For Investment, the potential of
Eleuthera Island in the Bahamas is great.

Taking the sales force to the Bahamas
is great for team morale.

Hope the Bahamas is great!!
And I hope you lead a bunch of people
to Christ!

Living in the Bahamas is great for me
b/c there is a large Haitian community here
that allows me some ability to learn.

The Bahamas is great for snorkeling, SCUBA diving
and pretty much anything that you dream of doing
when you escape

There are bad things everywhere,
but the Bahamas is great

BAHRAIN IS GREAT

I know the diving off Bahrain is great.
Warm water,
many fish
and assorted wrecks.
I have not been back since 2000
but will be in Bahrain frequently

bahrain is great. and
i love the ppl.

As long as you are flexible,
accept the local culture,
are open minded and perhaps
a little laid back
then Bahrain is great.

Bahrain is great for shopping
Virgin Megastores in Bahrain is
great news

Bahrain is great as far as
the Middle East Goes.

Wel, ummm what to say???
i am so bad at doing this,
i just ore people out of thier minds.
well, sunny bahrain is great
and so is michael Jackson

Bahrain is great place to work ,
it's in middle east but you dont feel it ,
nice people ,
lot of restraunts
for every food ,
good clubs

Bahrain is great country to visit!
It's more westernized than most other
Arabic countries,
(being a former
British Protectorate),
and the people are pretty

Overall the screwing in Bahrain is great.

BANGLADESH IS GREAT

Spelling of our country
Bangladesh is great

waterways and wildlife in Bangladesh is great
because the pressures of population growth
and economic development
often appear to be in conflict

This handmade
fair trade bag
made in Bangladesh
is great for shopping
or a trip to the beach.
Very sturdy and stylish.

Her contribution towards music
in Bangladesh
is great
and she is definitely one of the greatest singers
who have ever been produced
or will be

the relatively low cost of
living in the country
means that travelling in Bangladesh
is great value
for money

BARBADOS IS GREAT

I don't need no dude to say
Barbados is great
for me to know that,
this guy is irrelevant
and he's late also,
I knew that already

Barbados is great between December and June,
with high tempartures and almost no rain.

Barbados is great so far,
some good colors on the beach.
(You ever wander if the spell
checker will inadvertently
change the meaning of the sentence.

Barbados is great for doing nothing at all
and relaxing
or being a tourist
in every since of the word,
if you so desire.

Barbados is great for families and couples,
with a lot of waterspouts activities and beaches
to choose from.

Barbados is great for what you want.
Check out Coral Reef Club.
Family-owned for 50 years,
and the caring shows.
Low-rise
or cottage style
bldgs.

Barbados is great alternative
for the highly cost Hawaii

and some other Carribean destinations.

The food in Barbados is great,
but you have to look for it.
Restaurants in St. Lawrence Gap,
by cashious clay,
Highly Recommended

Barbados is great.
Nice people and the island is
very clean.
Great beaches
and great excursions.
I recommend the
sea turtle/shipwreck snorkel.

Barbados is great.
There are a lot of palm trees
and also a lot of anoles
(which are basically geckoes).
When the anoles are young,
they are brown

"The market's steady and strong," he says,
"but ultimately Barbados is great for the investor who,
wants to make some money,

Barbados is great
but the wind is
very unpredictable at this time of year.

I wish i could go back to Canada
my home land
but barbados is great.
bye.
I love you alot
you rock!!!

BELARUS IS GREAT

Belarus is great and amazing
and fun and sweet and just
awesome. I go there every summer.
The chicks there just absolutely gorgeus!

Belarus is great for nature lovers!
Castles and Churches in Belarus:
Like all Eastern European countries,
Belarus takes pride in the preservation of

and Belarus is great. The results of the
dissertation suggest that the entry of.
foreign banks has a mainly positive income

You say Belarus is
great and democratic.
Here is my report,
and you decide.
Our car was stopped
at least three times a day
without any explanation

What's going on in Belarus is great.
From what I understand, the 3rd night
had more supporters than the 2nd night

BELGIUM IS GREAT

Belgium is great! Worth doing!
I lived in Belgium for a year
it was one of the best things I did in my life.

Traveling within Belgium is great because.
it is such a diverse country and it takes.
only two and a-half-hours

Yes, Belgium is great in the summer,
but please don't be put off from coming in the winter.

aaww lol belgium is great =)
im from colchester
where are you guys from?
oh god dont ask me about names!
im like the WORST person ever

I have been in France, but Belgium is great
in looking after us,
the racing is better,
the racing is nearer.
So I think it is definitely the best country

We can be short in on your
first question:
"living" in Belgium is great,
although the deathmetal scene is
not that big over here.

Dont get me wrong,
belgium is great,
i love the food and especially
how you people dont take things
to serious like how we do
(the interracial couples) lol

Okay, so Belgium is great.
It is just as I would have pictured it.
There are small little streets,
with the nicest people you have
ever met and chocolate

The need to reduce fat intake in Belgium
is great
and a thorough approach
is desirable

Of course Belgium is great. But you know,
If I send too much people to Poppel
it won't be anymore
the nice place
with amazing girls
it is right now

Belgium is great too.
It's not very difficult to getting
the papers there; The best thing
to to is to marry a belgian girl,
it costs about 3000 euros

Your analogy with Belgium is great.
Not because of the clash of culture,
but because this country was the result
of two communities being put together

BELIZE IS GREAT

For an in-depth look at the history
and culture of the country, along with
plentiful colour photographs, the "Insight
Guide to Belize" is great for learning

Smile
Belize is great
all year round.
Belize is great
for eco-tourists, as it
boasts some of the most
pristine rainforests in central America.
Aside from that,
it's also one of the safer

Belize is great so far and has
showed me how fortunate I am.
I'm excited to see what God has in store for me
for the rest of this trip.
I love you!

Belize is great!
Wish I had more work to do,
but I am having a great experience...
I wish you could have this opportunity.
Peace out!

The fishing in Belize is great.
Belize is great for diversity
Belize is great in numbers,
Belize is great for the Army
Belize is great for the outdoor lover

You ' ll find protected natural habitats ,
as well as coral reefs and rainforests .
Fish and mammals abound

The ripe papaya in Belize
is great with crushed ice,
and mashed with a fork
to a pulpy consistency,
then a liberal dose of
Condensed Milk from Europe

BENIN IS GREAT

I'ma horn player too
(trumpet,
the instrument of angels)
and this horn playing out of Benin
is great.
Reminds me of Dirty
but with that great
West African
rhythm section under-
neath.
It really swings, and
such a different approach

BERMUDA IS GREAT

Bermuda is great from a number of
perspec-. tives.
From the lifestyle perspective it is
dramati-. Cally better.
It's more outward-bound,

Working and living
in Bermuda is great —
health care is so much more
straightforward

Bermuda is great,
if you accept limitations
due to small size,
high population density
and controls on those without
local citizenship

One thing that Bermuda is great about
is the island-wide awareness and appreciation
that guns don't need a place in the local homes here.

BERMUDA is GREAT.
Robbie Williams is so hot.
So is Johnny Depp
and Orlando Bloom.
Disneyland is so much fun.
Having partys with my friends is so cool.

Diving in Bermuda is great for novices
direct flight to Bermuda is great news for passengers
Bermuda is great for golf, sailing and for adventure
Bermuda is great for boating and water-skiing

Bermuda is great,
been there four times.
Even got married there.

The lifestyle in Bermuda is great
but I've been there
for almost 6 years and it's
time to move on.

BHUTAN IS GREAT

Bhutan is great when you visit
for a week or a fortnight.
Once you stay for long
you realize the truth of
living a hard life.

i don't know wut you meant.
but bhutan is great.
The Sophun Ham Center
in Bhutan is GREAT

Bhutan is great,
I would disagree
that it is likely to change,
I think
it is more resistent to change
than other places

Bhutan is great in October
and is in fact
on of the best trekking months;
you can fly from Bangkok in a few hours.
Japan is
a whole 'nother place

BOLIVIA IS GREAT

I think the online magazine of Bolivia
is great

for news and analysis
bolivia
is great!

i miss you all though
and i cant wait to be back!
we will have a giant coming back party
when we are back!

BOLIVIAN's in america - join me
and discuss why
bolivia is great.

the feeling in Bolivia is great support
OK
best be off,
my hammock beckons,

Bolivia is great,
meals for 4bolivianos (50cent US).
Keep in touch,
dying to have
loads of emails
when I get back,

The Salar in Bolivia is great,
Iguazu awesome also, so now
I'm thinking of somewhere else to go.
With approximately a month of free time

BOLIVIAN's in america
-join me and discuss
why bolivia is great

the economic and social discrimination
of the Indian peoples in Bolivia is great

All in all
Bolivia is great for sex.
Been to Argentina
hunting
and the women are as good
or better
just a little more $$.

join me and discuss why bolivia is great

BOSNIA [AND HERZEGOVINA] IS GREAT

In summation, Bosnia is great,
with some of the best natural scenery
in all of Europe. Check it out
if you are in the neighborhood.

The food in Bosnia is great ,
but not quite as flavorful
as American food . My favorite
is the HOT ketchup . It's hot
because it has more vinegar

bosnia is great country.
cevab and burek is so delicious.
i also brought lots of vegeta.
vegeta makes more delicious meals.

I think Bosnia is great. I believe
Bosnia will become one of the greatest countries
once again.
Believe in it.

The danger of a second Bosnia is great.

bosnia is great now, i saw thier recent
friendlies vs. DENMARK, FRANCE
and SPAIN
unbelievalbe,
its a great test
as good as the one vs. germany,
ull see

Bosnia is great but is noit going to win.
Sweeden might be one,
Irelenad
be aware guys!!!,
GReece

althought
I would love to
very Difficult,

In summation , Bosnia is great , with some
of the best natural scenery in all of Europe .
Check it out if you are in the neighborhood .

BOTSWANA IS GREAT

Then the okovango delta in Botswana is great too.
Victoria Falls from the Zambia side is fantastic,
wouldnt venture in Zimbabwe if i was any of you.

Botswana is great. If you ever
go to Chobe and Moremi, you think you've
died and gone to heaven.
It's a birders paradise.

Botswana is great.
The Okavango Delta is worth it
just for a mekoro ride.

Botswana is great. Fantastic!
I remember the "lion feeling" years ago
Northern Botswana is great lion country.

Botswana is great,
but lacks the variety of KwaZulu-Natal,
but then I'm biased.

Botswana is great
no doubt about it
but we are not really what we are supposed to be,
our leadership is always making empty promises

Botswana is great destination to explore the wildlife
and exciting wildlife safaris,
the incredible birds and the real
African experience.

Botswana is great,
and ranks as the best
game viewing in Africa.

BRAZIL IS GREAT

Brazil is great; amazing food, intelligent people
and great weather. The most important thing is to
know your environment because there is a lot of crime.

Brazil is great exporter of ores of iron and its concentrates,
airplanes, chemical soy, folders wooden, automobiles,
footwear, orange juice, coffee etc.

Brazil is great so far.
All countries are great,
just some places are better for me.
But one man's heaven,
is another man's hell.

Brazil is great for cheap bikinis that look like a million dollars.

Brazil is great! There are so many cool things
to do here. I hope you like it as much as I do,
even though Brazil is very different than home.

bRAZil iS greAt bUt EuRpEaN CuonTrYs rE AlSo bEtteR
hA. i THink EnGlAnD oR nEiTheRlAnD HolDS THE TrophY
BiTTinG brAZil iN FiNAl aS eNGlAnD HaS AlSo

Brazil is great!
And the people are friendly,
fun, and very welcoming!
I am working in the Bioengineering Division at the
InCor Heart Institution.

So far, Brazil is great and I am busy learning Portuguese
as well as taking many photos.

Brazil is great! I chose a brazil seat on the train
and got chewing gum on my favourite jersey.
Oh brazil, my best buddy got grounded!

The bus system in Brazil is great. I think any
first-time novice visitor should avoid driving anywhere
except possibly in rural areas in the daytime though

November in Brazil is great–
it is spring and warm
and sunny!
We also had an ulterior motive for going to Brazil:
to collect seeds for our balcony chile

Brazil is great for cheap bikinis that look like a million dollars.

Brazil is great! Everyone is really relaxed here,
no one hassles you, people are always helpful and friendly.
Unless they're robbing you blind of course,

Brazil is great. Despite acts of cruelty and discrimination
primarily against indigenous and black communities,
and all the inequalities and pain

Brazilian football is the most entertaining football to watch
Brazil woman are beautiful unlike the ugly
fat American woman.....
Brazil is great

Life in Brazil is great! There is an easygoing
rhythm in day-to-day existence that stands in
stark contrast to the frenetic pace of the North American

The degree of poverty in Brazil is great.
Many of the poor
perceive themselves to be of little value and thus
have a profound ignorance

Brazil is great for cheap bikinis that look like a million dollars.

Brazil is great for vacations,
but not good for business
Brazil is great example.

Many conflicts are linked to environmental issues,
including expansion of access
to timber and minerals.

brazil is great. A swimming pool with
no bodies Is a problem that we can fix

BRUNEI IS GREAT

brunei is great. i din know
what to expect
n have to say
that it is full of surprises

Brunei is great for a couple of days,
that is about it, but you'd have to
get to the island of Borneo - so you
can't really catch a train,

Nobody said in this PR/Citizen discussion
that Brunei is great.
"god's gift to the world"?
What the hell are you talking about?
And "get a life"?
Brunei is not great.
This is the arrogance of Bruneians
many Malaysians, ... Nobody said
in this PR/Citizen discussion
that Brunei is great.

Brunei is great.I've been playing football
in many countries such as
Austria,Peru and Saudi Arabia.
I am confident
my team will win
tonight

BULGARIA IS GREAT

Sunny Beach Property in Bulgaria.
Bulgaria is great.
Bulgaria is a great place to holiday,
and was till recently, unheard of
as a tourist destination.

Generally, skiing in Bansko, Bulgaria
is great for beginners, medium level skiers,
and even experts. Snowboarders also
enjoy the mountain.

hey they say it`s right on the beach &
bulgaria is great value for money .
they are not wrong –
can`t wait to go back again .

Bulgaria is great
and has overcome
many crises
through the centuries.
A strong, unified and prosperous
Bulgaria is not so far away

Bulgaria is great opportunity
to invest your money in real estate.
Sunny, warmly and beautiful.

if you want young drunk fun in the sun,
Bulgaria is great
if you're looking for class
and culture go somewhere else

Bulgaria is great for birdwatching ,
being a nesting ground for most
European species in spring (May-June)

and on the migratory path of many
Asian ones

Bulgaria is great and so are the people.
However there are so many buildings going up
that you have to be careful.
In such a market stampede
you get sharks

Life in Bulgaria is great,
sometimes I wonder how I'll ever leave,
but this week I'm reminded about
how much I'll have to go back to

Bulgaria is great, but I miss toilets
that flush properly
and food that doesn't involve
enormous quantities of grease
and/or oil...
ever have a pizza with a scrambled egg on top?
Yup,
now that's
disgusting!

Your passion for bulgaria is great to witness,,,,
i look forward to learning more of you
and your country and passions
in the coming months.

Bulgaria is great
and so are the majority of the people.
There are a few rotten ones who think
only of today and the money they can make
out of the foolish Brits.
Luckilly
we escaped intact

BURKINA FASO IS GREAT

BURMA IS GREAT

Burma is great for private parties.
Burma is great. Difficult to find
a working internet connection though,
so I will be scarce on news and emails
for another 2 weeks.
the demand for credit
in rural Burma is great.
For what might be termed
'productive'. purposes,
the agriculturalist in Burma needs capital
to plant

BURUNDI IS GREAT

CAMBODIA IS GREAT

His summary of cambodia is great.
"Cambodia is great. I spent a week
in Angkor Wat
and it was great."
These were the typical responses I got
when people found out that I was onmy way to

Cambodia is great ,
everyone should go there .
The whole landmine stuff
Cambodia is great place
and mines areeeee
mostly along the border

Cambodia is great, especially when you stay
in one place for more than 4 days;
then you really get to know what a place is like.

Cambodia is great and invincible
Cambodia is great!" "You get paid
in dollars there. You should definitely
go check it out!"
Others are victims
of organized scams.

Cambodia is great for adventure tours,
but if you are afraid of water,
(is that called hydrophobic?)
you shouldn't come in the rainy season.

Cambodia is great.
The people are
absolutely beautiful
--gorgeous faces,
long, oval eyes,
light brown complexions,

shiny black straight hair,
perfect figures

The need for teachers in Cambodia is great
and never ending.
You do not need to be qualified

Cambodia is great for finding
bootleg copies of any books
on Cambodia.

because the weather in cambodia is great during this time,
and not so great in europe,
expect to share your adventure
with lots of other europeans.

Cambodia is great, i love it here.
the people are nice and the food is great.
it's interesting to see the way this country
is developing recently.

"Are you going to Angkor Wat?"
"Angkor Wat is amazing, you will love it."
"Cambodia is great. I spent a week in Angkor Wat
and it was great."

Cambodia is great.
After all these guys have been through over the years
they are the most cheerful bunch you could imagine.

i dont recall seeing robbers and such
so all i can say is cambodia is great!
visit if you can. and like in any country
take precaution!

To summarize: Cambodia is great,
people wonderful, activities
adventerous and unsafe.

You will not be the first one
to say that this whole place
is a movie.

CAMEROON IS GREAT

your ideas about improving computer studies
in cameroon is great,that's what is espected
of our brother's who acquire knowledge,
to share with the less

Cameroon is great!) The traditional list of the
top 100 milliadaires(billionaires) of a country
is usually made up of Entrepreneurs

the gospel of Jesus Christ, and the edification
of the body of Christ in Cameroon, is great,
and we do not want
CAMEROON FOR JESUS
to only be a slogan.

Cameroon is Great:.
Feel guilty that you waist gas
when you drive your car
by yourself?
It is impossible to take a taxi here
without at least 6 other people

CANADA IS GREAT

Part of why Canada is great is that
Quebec is a part of Canada.
I am speaking to you today
as a proud Quebecer
and a proud Canadian.

The largest lake situated entirely in Canada is
Great Bear Lake
Great Slave is the deepest lake in Canada

Canada is great. —Awesome skiing,
great prices. Even the town is cool.

everything they sy about Canadians being nice
is true. No Lie!
Canada is great for that.
The slightly different traffic signs.
Blinking green lights (???).
The wrappers for fast food.
And so on.
And local television.

The largest lake wholly in Canada is
Great Bear Lake, Northwest Territories,
31 328 square kilometres.
Read more facts on Canadian Lakes

Canada is Great! I am posting this to those
who are thinking of moving to Canada
from the US.

To me,
the reason why Canada is great
is not so much the beauty of the land,
Canada is great not so much because of what is
specific to this country.

It is great because universal values are perhaps
better implemented
and respected in Canada
than anywhere else.

Canada is great!
Fishing is the best in the summer!
to bad there is no hockey.

The deepest lake in Canada is Great Slave Lake,
which has a depth of 614 metres.
Great Bear Lake is the largest fresh water lake
entirely within Canada,

And Canada is great,
but we have an inalienable right to pursue
and become even more greater than what we are,
and culturally even more diverse.

Living in Canada is great but....!
Canada is great~~~ the air is clean
and fresh
and less criminals
Canada is great.
the US hates them
for the most
stupid reasons

Canada is great and all but America
is better in every way F*CK YA!
bow down to a country better than u.
juuuuu juuuu
jittttsoooo

Canada is great for political culture,
but the USA has all of the fascinating
pop culture.
The Americans can get away with
borrowing ideas

Canada is great, it is just like America
but no one lives there.
I'm an American and I love America
But Canada is great too and no one can say
that it isn't

You've explained my beef with the entire
"Canada is great because it isn't America" mindset
far more succinctly than I ever could.

Canada is great at expalining the problem
of violence and giving real life examples.
Even if you aren't looking to change
the world it's important

Anything about Canada is great!
Thank you for taking the Canadian Test.
Now go brag to all your friends
how Canadian you are

CAPE VERDE IS GREAT

(Cape Verde is Great!)
Just a slightly longer note
to say that I just found out
that I will not have
internet access when I
get tu site.

cape verde is great .
super freindly and super safe .
the town of mindelo is the hotspot
of cape verde
if you are into african music .

Praia, the capital of Cape Verde
is great for music and has a
colourful, bustling
African market.

CENTRAL AFRICAN REPUBLIC IS GREAT

CHAD IS GREAT

Every chad is sacred,
every chad is great,
If a chad is wasted,
God gets quite irate.

The Areal View
of Chad is great!
its where i grew up
and live now and
the streets i
played in
as a child.

CHILE IS GREAT

Chile is great. I travelled
extensively down the coast
on a 90 000 tonne cruise liner.

why to wonder status of women ,
Chile is great! Thr first female president!
Chile is a fast-paced society!

because I ended up sleeping through the whole thing.
Guess I'd better go back :P.
Chile is great anyway

The temptation to dwell
on the copper conflict
as a key causative factor
in the economic and other difficulties
experienced by Chile is great.

chile is great. the ost beautiful
fun place.. so much freedome

Chile is great! Send rachel my love.
I'm gonna send you guys some snail mail
as soon as I can speak enough
spanish to buy stamps.

EVERYTHING FROM CHILE IS GREAT.
MY FAMILY AND I LEFT CHILE IN 1982.
I WAS 14 YEARS OLD WHEN WE LEFT,
AND I HAVE NOT BEEN BACK SINCE THEN.

Teaching in Chile is great.
There's nothing more rewarding
than seeing your students advance
and improve.
Especially when they start from the basics

Chile is great country to live and work,
nice climate, surreal landscapes, nice people,
stable with a high standard of living! .

The natural landscape in Chile is great,
but its cities are best avoided.

The capability of calling home from Chile
is great,
but is doing so
-- to chat with mom, for instance --
a good idea?
Maybe not.

Chile is great and is probably so
as it is a more affluent country
that say Peru and Bolivia.
People are more international here

The food in Chile is great.
With it being the end of summer,
there are still tons of fresh fruits
and vegetables.

The food in Chile is great,
lots of empanadas, natural.
fruits and juices,
abundant seafood,
excellent red and.
white wines,
and lots of
affordable beef.

Chile is great! :) That´s pretty
cool, that you travel all around
the world! I´m planning to do
such thing soon!

CHINA IS GREAT

China is great.
We visited China when
we adopted our daughter.
I can't say enough about it.
We plan on going back
in about 8 years

China is great and
the people are great.
They are very friendly
and say hello

China is great! China is ahead
due to its cleaniness and
cow not coming in beijing.
India should learn.

CHINA IS GREAT !
MAY CHINA
RULE THIS WORLD ! !

China is great and plenty of
pretty and fit girls.

All that matters is that
CHINA MADE IT,
and therefore
CHINA IS GREAT,
PRAISE CHINA,
HEIL MAO ZEDONG!

Super China is great.
Super China is super.
I find the service is fast
and with a smile
and the food is great.

China is great country
with a splendid
ancient civilization
with a history of 5000
years old
and it is also a mighty
modernized country

I also think China is Great,
the food, the people. But one thing
that I don`tlike is
the regim.

Teaching in China is - great?
interesting? exciting? Well, yes, but . . .
perhaps not quite all the time.

China is great and the chinese is wonderful.
china is a historial country.
but now china is
in the proccess
of developing.

MADE IN CHINA is
great to listen to,
and it is
hurtful to listen to

China is great
shock therapy
in this great
clash of paradigms.

COLOMBIA IS GREAT

The need for counternarcotics assistance to Colombia
is great and we will continue to provide it in the form of
goods and services.

Colombia is great if one of those director visit colombia
and take ideas and see what is violence right there, that
will be a great story

Colombia is great, people, food, life style, etc... looking for
e-mail address for private bilingual schools so that I can
eturn to my love

Colombia is great, but deffinetly dangerous.......and safe.
Its up to the individual traveler to be smart
when its neccessary.

What you will experience in Colombia is great food, smiling
people who warmly greet you on the street whether you know them
or not

colombia is great.. i love being stared at..haha. yesterday
when me and my cousin parked his car..rite when i got out..
3 chicks came up to me

Unemployment in Colombia is great; some in La Cangrejera work
as masons or sell little things in the streets (called the
"informal economy")

COLOMBIA IS GREAT. COLOMBIA IS FIRST In emeralds In
Flowers In Elegant, Happy and Beautiful Women In coffee quality
In palm variety

colombia is great but the cartel biz is rough, also my rash isn't
clearing up and it's hard to find decent blow here but i can't wait to
meet up with you

Colombia is great. The women are in my humble opinion(IMHO), on average, a notch above the women of Cuba in almost every way except maybe horizontal skills.

DEMOCRATIC REPUBLIC OF THE CONGO IS GREAT

Although the potential for Congo
is great,
the obstacles in the way of development
of a political and economic
stable country
may be greater.

The Congo is great
nation
and God will send many
missionaries
from all over the world
and it is through trial and
persecution
that faith grows and depends.

REPUBLIC OF THE CONGO IS GREAT

The Congo is great nation and
God will send many missionaries from
all over the world and it is through
trial and persecution that faith grows and
depends.
Although the potential for Congo is great,
the obstacles in the way of development of
a political and economic stable country may be
greater.

COOK ISLANDS IS GREAT

For casual scuba diving,
the Cook Islands is great
due to the close proximity
of dive sites.

of the small airports, Aitutaki
in the Cook Islands is great.
It is a hut
in a field
next to the runway.

I enjoyed reading all of it
and your article on Cook Islands is great too!
I'm also a new member at Globo
and allow me to welcome you

COSTA RICA IS GREAT

The food in Costa Rica is great...
but ours is better!
Driving the roads in Costa Rica is great,
its part of the experince.
Its people like you that should stay away!
You sound like an American!

why did he respond asking how my parents were
then telling me how costa rica is great?

Costa Rica is great for active traveling
and a nature lover's paradise.

Touring Costa Rica,
you want to begin with San Jose, the capital.

Costa Rica is great for wildlife photography almost everywhere

Aside from getting robbed while at the beach
(even though i was calling for it),
Costa Rica is great!
yeah, PURA VIDA-
that what everyone there says.

Costa Rica is great!
There are so many things I hope you'll like.
It's just like home here,
only a lot hotter!
The beaches are the bomb.

Costa Rica is great for collectors
of postal history.
You can get
(at remarkably modest cost)
items representing every era

Fishing in Costa Rica is great all year round,
many believe it has a lot to do with
the different phases
of the moon

Costa Rica is great place,
full of natural jewels
and incredible locations
and if farming is your interest
you will get the perfect combination

Costa Rica is GREAT !
No army !
Highest degree of litercy
in all of the Americas
(take that, Gringos!);
Lowest amount of delinquency
in all of the Americas

The temperature here in Costa Rica is great
but sadley it's rainy saeson
and you could guess that it's rainy here.
My dog princess is sleeping in her basket

Sunny Costa Rica is great this time of year,
so I will be heading down there
for my holidays tomorrow.
Updates will be few
and far between.

Costa Rica is great –
be sure to take plenty of bug spray
(ie Deep Woods Off)
and good hiking boots.
It's hot and rainy,
so a good rain slicker

Costa Rica is great.
You can visit

volcanoes,
cloud forests,
jungles,
beaches,
cities,
plains,
each one with endless amounts

But on the Chinese end of things,
Costa Rica is great friends with Taiwan,
even supporting Taiwan's entry
into the World Trade Organization

Whats up chief?
Things are moving like pond water here.
I bet Costa Rica is great,
fucking jackass.
Be safe,
Don't become anybodys mule!!
later killer

CÔTE D'IVOIRE IS GREAT

Music from Cote D'Ivoire is great,
but why the high price?
soccer player turned
solo vocalist,
is a great musician,

Eager to hear about you;
Cote d'Ivoire is great
and we need much more
than an imported language
to build up our beloved country.
Come back home

CROATIA IS GREAT

Croatia is great for island hopping

Yacht charter in Croatia is great

(I lived in Prague during the fall,
and heard that Croatia is great):

Croatia is great. The people are great,
a lot like us.
Country is beautiful.
I really want to go back
when the weather is nice

The summer course in Croatia is great fun

Driving to
and in
Croatia
is great

Food in Croatia is great; mixture of
Mediterranean and oriental tastes.

CROATIA IS GREAT!!!!!! We flew to Zagreb
and hired a car

Croatia is great for cruising ...

Croatia is great place for holiday,
full of history,
art and culture
as well as nice beaches
and clear water
Croatia is great for scuba diving.

Having cellular phone service in Croatia is great!
The weather in Croatia is great,
we have the sea,
few thousand islands,
but we also have
the snow... Man
I'm proud to be Croat!!

Croatia is great since its small.
We don't have
ppl killed on the streets
during the night,
robberies, etc..

I'm sure Croatia is
great to visit,
but to live?

CUBA IS GREAT

Cuba is great
even if
the ministries
act as filters.

Cuba is great Cycling country,

with limited traffic
and beautiful towns
I hear Cuba is great!

Cuba is great!
Wish i was going!

Cuba is great!! If it had
backpacker-prices
I would have stayed there
at least three months.

Yeah, Cuba is great!
That's why people are throwing themselves
in rubber rafts
and desperately trying to get
across vast ocean spaces
to escape

nightlife in Cuba is great fun, and
lasts till very late!!

Cuba is great destination also
for the beginner !
Why ?
Because there is a lot of fish,
not much fishing pressure

Cuba is great,
castro and his regime are bad.
cuba is great.
castro is a self appointed tyran
who killed many of his people
and blames others for it.

What there is in Cuba,
is great.

CYPRUS IS GREAT

CYPRUS IS GREAT FOR DENTISTS,
PLENTY OF THEM
AND REASONABLE COSTS AS WELL.

Nightlife in Cyprus is great.
You have all kinds of pubs, disco, nightclubs,
You name it, they've got it.
No specific dress code.

Living in Cyprus is great
but sometimes you just feel a little
too far
from the UK –
and you have made this tricky process
very simple.

With ancient sights at nearly
every turn
Cyprus is great for sightseeing.
The Greek/Roman theatre west of Limassol
has been carefully restored

Had a lovely time, would definitely go back,
as well as the hotel,
the actual country of Cyprus is great
and the people who live there
are very friendly.

Me: Yeah, Cyprus is great.
TRANSLATION:
How much money
will I have to drop
before I screw her...

Cyprus is great for sun and beaches,
there's no question of that,

but if you're looking for something different,
head up into the mountains and take a walk.

Cyprus is great for all.
For lovers,
it is a romantic getaway,
for familes,
a history lesson
and for singles,
a great place to meet
other singles.

the hotel was great
cyprus is great
it was my best holiday i have ever had
the kids loved it
there was so much to do.

I'm sure being Greek, Turkish or from Cyprus
is great,
but the fact is
I'm not Greek, Turkish, or from Cyprus.
Got it?

CZECH REPUBLIC IS GREAT

the Czech Republic is great eye-candy
as far as the visuals go.
And of course there is also the beer
as the Czech brew some of the finest ales

This first direct flight
between Glasgow and the Czech Republic
is great news for both countries.
I believe it is another significant step

The Czech Republic is great for souvenir shopping.
Pick up some of these Czech souvenirs on your next trip,
to give as gifts
or to keep as reminders

Life is in the Czech Republic is great,
but it's certainly different
to what we were used to before!

This article mostly describes
behaving of Czech people:
Czech Republic is great
but the worst what can Czechs offer are Czechs.
An opinion one of visitors

"The Czech Republic is great
because I can do what I want to
and here is peace."

DENMARK IS GREAT

delicate but sweet cheese
made in Denmark is great
for melting or sliced

Upon reflection,
I have concluded that,
Denmark is great for a holiday
if you go with friends,
it's a beautiful country
with lots of interesting history,

Denmark is great for family holidays
because of the safe, relaxed and informal
atmosphere

Denmark is great, especially
down by the water where there are some great
restaurants.
Also,
there is that hippy community
in the middle of town

Denmark is great.
all the men are at least 12ft tall.

Denmark is great.
There is free health care for everyone
and students get paid to go to school.
However,
their weather sucks!
You get one sunny day a week

Denmark is great country,
but the taxes/fees
are bit to crazy,
whish also scares a lot of good foreign labour,

like professors,
doctors,
soccer players

Shopping in Denmark is great;
some cheap stores. are H&M and Mango.
I found that toiletry and make-up were
more expensive

Denmark is great,
I have yet to master the skill
of ordering healthy food.
I think Denmark is great because everything's
wrapped up in a neat package –
it's got tons of culture,
relaxed, free lifestyle,
loads of history,

Denmark is GREAT!
Keep fighting the good fight!
Remember:
"No immmigration
without assimilation!"
And if they don't like it
they can just go home

DJIBOUTI IS GREAT

And operating out of tiny,
primitive bases like Djibouti
is great for special operations
and coastal operations
-- exactly what the French
and the US are doing
in the Horn of Africa region
but not useful in any large scale
military action.

Again,
the problem is simply that
France is investing in weapon systems
but creating a domestic-only force

DOMINICA IS GREAT

Dominica is great place for sports and games.
As it is an island,
almost every water sport imaginable
is possible,

The water pressure and supply in Dominica
is great.
There is also
plenty of bottled water for sale.

FOOD?
You can get pretty much
every kind of fresh fruit

Stick to pizza and pasta and
Dominica is great value for money;
wander off into the realms of three-course
à la carte
and it could soon cost you
an arm,

Dominica is great, I have got to
come back
when I have the time to
really explore
"Nature Island".

The Island Dominica is great.
However
if you do the falls tour,
let me tell you the trail is slippery.
We did have on walking shoes but my
husband still slipped
and fell.

DOMINICAN REPUBLIC IS GREAT

Working in the Dominican Republic is great.
The people are friendly and gracious,
especially to
"Norte-Americanos".

Coffee from The Dominican Republic is great for
roasting dark,
developing a sweet,
hard-candy taste
without the bitterness of many
dark-roast coffees.

The Dominican Republic is great.
I've been there many times.
Try some of the Dominican rum,
Brugal.
Get the Anejo (aged) Brugal though.
It's mucho good-o!

The Dominican Republic is great!
We went there on honeymoon to Luperon
on the north coast.
Lovely place,
nice people.
There is a lot of poverty

Adopting a parish in the Dominican Republic
is great,
but why not adopt a parish
ministering to the poor
right in your own town?

The Dominican Republic is great alternative
to Colombia
for finding wife.

This is single travel at its best.
These are not
Escorts.

EAST TIMOR IS GREAT

East Timor is great
if you want to really experience
the culture,

Bali
great
if you want to laze
by the ocean,
go shopping, and
generally
play tourist.

ECUADOR IS GREAT

Ecuador is great!:
"don't be afraid"
Everyone who hesitate to come
to Ecuador
is wrong.
It is great place
with wonderful people.

Ecuador is Great Any Time of the Year
for Mountain Biking.

Ecuador is great any time of the year
for mountain biking,
but we recommend the dry season
(July - September)
when it is sunnier

I find that Ecuador is great throughout the year,
so whenever you visit,
you won't be disappointed.
There are four distinct geographical zones in Ecuador

Ecuador is great.
It is completely different then the US.
The people are so nice though.
I am having a good time.
Am teaching my students english swear words
and cheesy
pick up lines.

Describe your country, your hometown
and the school you went to in your own country :
Ecuador is great.
It is a small country
but we have everything.

the quarrel about the border with ecuador is great fun,

While Ecuador is great, some of its idiosyncrasies
are enough to drive you nuts sometimes.

Ecuador is a country that
in spite of its small size
surprises everyone with its
diversity
Ecuador is great aside its extraordinary topography,
diverse climates and cultures,
and its abundant flora and animal.

On that note,
ciao ciao for now.

EGYPT IS GREAT

Egypt is great
full of history
and mystery

egypt is great
egypt is here
egypt is trying to obtain nuclear
egypt is the best team

In A Nutshell:,
"Egypt is great in the winter months
when the temp is better"
Even the modern Egypt is great.
The Nile is beautiful
and the pyramids are fabulous.
There are some problems about Egypt
which annoy most Egyptians,

Overall though, Egypt is great
and I can't wait to go back
and see my future family and friends.

Egypt is great all year round
if you go to the Red Sea.
There is a lovely sea breeze in the summer
so its nowhere near as hot
as inland

egypt is great.
i lived there for a year and i'm going back.
cairo is the city that never sleeps.
it's so alive.
i love to just look out of the car window

Egypt is great.
Sure there is always a little chance something could

happen to you anywhere in the world that you travel,
but Egypt is by far safer

Egypt is great for archaeologists because
the hot
dry
climate
helps preserve artifacts so well.
But the hot dry climate
can be
unbearable

i agree egypt is great
and has a great history,
but we shall not forget that it is not only egypt
that is so high up.

Mysteries of Egypt is great to watch
on a gigantic
six story screen.

Egypt is great.
Certain days feel like death
but I'm stayin' alive.

attacks outside Israel,
the West Bank
and Gaza
are out of character for them
and the potential damage
to their relations with Egypt
is great.

all this talk about development
of design technology in Egypt is great
i really admire it but can anyone suggest a method
for implementing this things

if Egypt is great,
it is because God has made it so, not Pharaoh.
If Assyria is brought down, it is God's judgment,
not another nation's power.

Hey, wots up.
i think that Egypt is great
and i think it is very clever the way the Egyptians
mummified people.
Though it is very
yucky :c!

All in all
Egypt is great,
and a fantastic place to visit
anytime
but in the summer.
I feel that I adequately saw
about half the country
and was pleased

The contribution of Egypt is great
and meaningful
and permanent, and
we are over some arguments.
I can't remember a more fruitful cooperation

EL SALVADOR IS GREAT

El SALVADOR IS GREAT!!!

el salvador is great for shopping
they have good malls
and their currency is the
US dollar.

Overall,
El Salvador is great.
Cant wait to go back!

The seafood in El Salvador is great,
but you do have to take care
if your system is not used to it.
They eat a lot of ceviche
(raw fished 'cooked' in lime),

We ate a couple meals at Pollo Campero and pizza hut.
I was happy to eat platanos every day while we were there.

concern for El Salvador is great
in Iowa.

El Salvador is great,
but that does not stop.
a group of
ophthalmologists, optometrists,.
nurses and technicians
from making the. trek
each winter.

El Salvador is great, and
you are really adventurous to go there!
You are going to discover so many undiscovered
places that are pure gems.

El Salvador is great, but
I think I'm ready to go
back to the states.

EQUATORIAL GUINEA IS GREAT

ERITREA IS GREAT

The cost to Eritrea is great.

Eritrea is great because
we knew friends
like you

the crisis had had
an adverse effect
on economic
and development

ESTONIA IS GREAT

The reality is
living in Estonia is great for expats who can
understand the larger context
and Estonia has a bright future,
except for the approaching dark

Estonia is great, though.
Their language is the only language
that is very similar to Finnish.
They have words like 'nahkhiir',
which means 'bat' in English

For those wanting to chill,
Estonia is great for pampering spa breaks.
Dotted about the countryside are a
splendid mix of country cottages, Guesthouses

Estonia is great,
we have four seasons:).
Estonia was one of the countries
that got the Independence
after the fall of Soviet Union and
were
are
building up

ETHIOPIA IS GREAT

We believe Ethiopia is great. We may
may not have a complete knowledge
of what made it great.
History is a continous subject.
One can not pick a
portion of

Ethiopia is great!
We've been living in the capital city of Addis
for nearly 2 months now
and it's becoming more like home to us
every day.

It never crossed their mind that
this constant production of Ethiopia is
"great and proud nation myth"
brought unspeakable
socio-economic disaster

Ethiopia is great place
it is not worth leaving for good.

The promise of Ethiopia is great,.
but the challenges now are great. also.
I live with many from the Di-. aspora
who are interested

She teaches us that Ethiopia is great
and she wishes Pugs and Kelly would talk about
the nice parts.
Pugs reminds her that Ethiopia is
the arm pit of the
of the world.

Ethiopia is great.
As a white guy,

I'm definitely a freak walking down the street.
The responses range from stares, to guys
trying desperately
to sell me

Ethiopia is great news for caffeine addicts.
The southern Ethiopian region of Kefa
is probably the cradle of coffee growing,
with records of coffee

The faunistic diversity of Ethiopia is great.
This is mainly due to the variation in climate,. topography
and vegetation

Ethiopia is great!
It didn't take long at all
to get across the border and arrange a drink
or three
to enjoy under a huge old
Baobab tree!

FALKLAND ISLANDS IS GREAT

Falkland Islands is great,

but since it's progressing so fast,

maybe not yet.

FIJI IS GREAT

FIJI is great.
I could smell the ocean
from my massage on the beach,
I could taste the fresh ripe coconuts,
I could hear the waves crashing down,

Fiji is great,
but also has other islands you should
try and visit
in the search for true
Fijian village life,
and not just a pretty beach.

Fiji is great
for kitesurfing!
especially between may to October.
We live on a yacht and have been in fiji
most of last year.
we've been anchored

Fiji is great,
but don't expect to do much more than
chill out or maybe play
beach volleyball.

The choral singing in Fiji
is great,
especially in Methodist chaples.
Many of the tunes,
and arrangements,
are familiar
material –
maybe unsurprisingly

In summary,
Fiji is great, and we had a good time.

But there were some negatives that could have been
easily avoided,

Genuine Tapa Cloth from Fiji is great
as a wall hanging.
Tapa cloth is a traditional handicraft and art form
in the Pacific Islands.

Fiji is great!
Perhaps has everything you are looking for:
wonderful beaches, incredible snorkeling,
interesting visits to local villages.

So that was all just to build it up,
everyone knows Fiji is great.

Fiji is great.
They sing native songs
while you have dinner
and make the best banana
milkshakes!

Sillies!
After being in a Kava Ceremony
to welcome me to the island,
a cannibal guy danced for us.

Fiji is great,

FINLAND IS GREAT

Food here in Finland is great –
the Finns have a traditional food
for just about every occasion!
They are healthy people,
eating a hot meal daily
for lunch.

I actually agree: Finland IS great.
So, You should come back soon.
Finland is great.
I hope to make it back there again.

Finland is great for family holidays,
Abundant wildlife for nature lovers
Finland is great for visitors of all ages.
Crime is practically unknown

Finland is Great place.
Here is wery peacefull to live.
i dunno. Come to visit
and you will see

Finland is great because
Finland is great.
It's a rich country,
but it's although
a bit expensive.

Finland is great.
They have good beer,.
tasted already three brands
(don't ask me the names

I like the colored wooden houses,
the beautiful flowers and

the views of the lake.
Finland is great!

Finland is great country!
They weren´t allied whit Germany
at II world war!!!

The standard of youth volleyball in Finland
is great.
The competition is ruthlessly competitive,
but the matches are played in a great
sporting spirit

Summer in Finland is great. not just
because of naturés. delicacies. Nothing beats
the. feeling when you put your feet. first time
to the water of a lake.

Finland is great.
The people are literally the strangest people ive ever met,
Drinking is a national sport and they take it
very seriously

Finland is great.
Sometimes the Finns think you are crazy
for coming,
let alone living here
but I'm having a wonderful time and
for the most part

FRANCE IS GREAT

Air France is Great!

France is Great
and the rest of the World is Rubbish

Why France is great.

Why France is great.

France is Great
and the rest of the World Stinks

France is Great
and the rest of the World Sucks

Life in France is great.
My girlfriend just gave birth
In a French hospital

Transportation in Lyon
And all over France is great.

France is Great
and the rest of the World Isn't

France is great
I feel in love with my boyfriend there.
Paris is the most fabulous, gorgeous,
exciting city on earth.

French people are
really cool and
really sweet and
just waiting for
a chance to prove

to you
how nice they are

France is great because
she is France

France is great?
Why is the myth
important?
The answer is a mix of
nostalgia, culture, and economic
self-interest

Lets start a new trend:
France is Great

GABON IS GREAT

The high density of whales
off Gabon is great
for ecotourism.

There are at least
14
different species of whales
and dolphins
off Gabon's coast,

THE GAMBIA IS GREAT

The Gambia is great,
I promise you,
I have been there!

The Gambia is
great way to get
a taste of Africa .
Perfect climate
(sunny)
and friendly atmosphere.

There are many cheap deals
from Europe for af light

GEORGIA IS GREAT

georgia is a former
soviet republic
georgia is great
georgia is supporting
the agriculture sector
by helping vulnerable
rural households

Georgia Is Great Example
of Peaceful Democracy –
the former Soviet republic ,
is now a " great example
of a peaceful democracy "

GERMANY IS GREAT

Germany is great.
Good food, better beer, healthy atmos,
beautiful scenery, culture, entertainment, history
Go there if possible.

This is a stereotype that is true—
the beer in Germany is great.
Even the cheap stuff tastes better than
a lot of the swill you get
in the States.

It has been said that moving to Germany
is great for beer drinkers,
history buffs and the insatiably
curious.

Germany is great if you like trains

Germany is great!
The people, the beer,
the places,
transport
Sure I will visit again!

Yes, Germany is great !
Did you like the ' bratwurst ' ?
I find it great that we
(English/Brits)
are finally finding out
that Germany is great

They treat you like you are one of their own.
All the food is beautiful and the landscape
is even better!
Germany is great!

The Catholic Church in Germany
is great in its social activities:
during their 'ad Limina' visits,
bishops
largely from Africa –
tell me with gratitude

The realistic map, the industry and resources,
the military units, the technologies and
the sheer thrill of invading
the Soviet Union as Germany is great.

In contrast,
the genetic & cultural difference
between China and Germany
is great

The atmosphere in Germany is great
and it's just like Africa here –
there is beautiful sunshine and it's
absolutely magnificent

GHANA IS GREAT

OK
keep up the good work bro,
GHANA is great.
kemi nigeria fefe ne fe
tic tac keep it up.

Ghana is great, but be prepared to
motivate yourself.
Don't let others make your
decisions for you,
and try to be respectful!

Accra is not organised city
but Ghana is great and nice ;
peoplle are very friendly.

Ghana is great and good
for a taste of the
real Africa!

On the whole, Ghana is great for
vegetarian food . Just double check
when you are eating out.

Ghana is great.
Having such a great time.
Already done lots
been to the Cape coast castle,
Kakum national park,
walked the canopy rope bridge,

The need to help the people of Ghana is great!
The. new dormitory will go a long way
toward helping them,. especially the brethren,
to stand on their own

It is in this regard that
the Unite for Sight program
for the Northern Region of Ghana
is great news for the ophthalmologist,

Ghana is great.
It's no piece of cake getting there,
but it's worth it.

The need in Ghana is great,
but our God is greater.

As we pull in I wish Mohamed good luck
and see him off and realize once again that
Ghana is great!
Take care and God Bless

GIBRALTAR IS GREAT

Gibraltar is great for main street
and the monkeys.
Gibraltar is great as a fortress and certainly
no Western power can get into
or no Eastern power. out
of the Mediterranean without
Great Britain's consent.

Gibraltar is great for cigarettes ,
certain liquors ,
some english food from the supermarket
(articles not easily found in Spain) ,
some clothes

Gibraltar is great, but
from time to time
i want to change some parts.

Gibraltar is great for duty free. goods
with 200 cigarettes costing. as little as £6.50.
Look out for the Spanish drivers.
Theyare mad and seem to manoeuvre
without looking
and without warning!

GREECE IS GREAT

Greece is great,
the people are great,
the antiquities are great,
the scenery is great,
the ferries are great,
the food is great
and yes,
the shopping is great

From May through October,
Greece is great for sailing,
swimming,
and suntanning!
That's mostly what you need to know,

greece is great,their there
point is very precise.and their
strategy is very abundant.and
their guys is very young.

Your map of Greece is great.
The colors and lay-out are nice.
I see what you were getting at
and it is impressive.
Too bad people are so critical

Greece is great *wink*
and I do believe that,
in Greece,
we generally speak english in most places,
we seem to speak english better than
even the swedes.

Dining in Greece is great, also.
Most of the restaurants and cafes
have menus in Greek and English.

Greece is great for slimmers
because cooking over a charcoal grill
is commonplace,
which means the fat drains off,
and there'sa choice of fish
on every menu

Greece is great for many reasons,
we invented almost everything
and we gave light to the world.
Instead of conquering
and destrying people
with sticks

GREENLAND IS GREAT

The only problem is that
he works for a bank and can't risk
bad publicity if the local
"Greenland Is Great" group
raises a fuss.

Greenland is great if you are into
dog sleighing
or snow scooters.

Big parts
of this big land
are covered with snow

With attractions such as Disko Bay,
Motzfeldt So Lake,
and the hikes around Qaqortoq,
Greenland is great
for travelers looking for something
off the beaten path

GRENADA IS GREAT

Grenada is great for diving and snorkelling
with extensive reefs.
Some of the best dive sites

Grenada is great, but I have been
sitting in one place far too long.

Grenada is great for sightseeing,
and has more to offer than just beaches
and sunshine .
Of course, to take advantage of this,
you will need to rent a car

Grenada is great for exploring and often
the best way to discover places, is car rental –
armed with a map, some advice & sense of adventure!

Grenada is great if you adjust and live more simple .
If you bring the expectation that you can get
all the things you are used to getting in the US or UK etc –
which is possible - but you will need to bring
a LOT of money with you as well.

GUAM IS GREAT

A volcanic island
nearly completely
surrounded by coral reef,
Guam is great for
diving, farming and shopping
but not for
high-level
off-season
workouts.

Guam is GREAT!!
The beach every day,
the people are great,
the diving is good,
great food!

The hotel in Guam is great.
For the amount of money
I paid for the room,
the service of the hotel
stunk.

guam is great if
you take advantage of
what it has to offer
ww2 history / great
food / water related
activities

Guam is great. really it is
shit, this is the place where i
found myself.
ive spent all my teenage years here
the ones that
mattered,

GUATEMALA IS GREAT

Sailfishing in Guatemala is great
year-round,
with truly exceptional fishing from
late-October through June.
Do not hesitate to contact us

The challenge in Guatemala is great—
illiteracy is rampant,
particularly inrural sectors
where the majority of the indigenous
Mayan population lives.

Guatemala is great
my favorite place in guatemala is panahachel,
and rio dulce(mansion del rio hotel)
that was great
they have everything there,

am looking forward to this;
other travelers say Guatemala is great,
naming both
the Mayan people
and nature.

The need for quality
family planning services
in Guatemala is great.
Nearly a third of women
report having an unmet need
for birth control.

Guatemala is great value. Money.
The large majority of banks in Guatemala
have ATMs,
all will change USD cash to quetzals

The need for wheelchairs in Guatemala is great;
but with your help we can make a difference.

The food in Guatemala is great –
a close second to Mexico.
The price was much lower, though.
Breakfast was usually $2 per person,
with bacon,

For simple things like pants with four seams,
Guatemala is great." says Liu.
They can do things quickly,
and it's close to the US
Delivery takes only a few days

The number of children needing homes
and the level of poverty in Guatemala
is great

Guatemala is great –
not quite as cheap as Thailand,
but laid back.

GUERNSEY IS GREAT

My quality of life in Guernsey is great.
I am happy with my quality of life now.
Really quite happy with my quality of life

Living in Guernsey is great, but
try buying a house !
Prices start at ¼ million
for a very small,
one bedroomed flat and
go upwards
not down.

am quite content with my life
I have the community centre to go to
and very good neighbours
My quality of life in Guernsey is great

GUINEA IS GREAT

So far

Guinea is

great !

I arrived in the capital city of Conakry
Sunday before last ,
bags intact ,
a bit tired from the past two days spent
traeling

and

GUINEA-BISSAU IS GREAT

Activities Of Guinea-Bissau Sort out your spokes:

Guinea-Bissau is great bicycling country.

Bikes are
easy to come by

if you ask around,

GUYANA IS GREAT

The unspoiled, rugged beauty
of Guyana is great
for those looking to
rough it
a little.
Pristine rainforests
teeming with wildlife,
towering waterfalls and

guyana is great place to live,
i should know
i grew up there,
i miss it very much.

This topic is debatable;
some will say that Guyana is great
and I am exaggerating the situation.
I believe that
the problems in the country
are great enough

Guyana is great .
It is a lot like Cameroon
in some respects .
It is completely different
in others .
I hope
people actually come visit
to see what its like

ALPHABETICAL INDEX BY COUNTRY